Lizard Reality

Indigo Dreams II

Ronnie Goodyer

To Hannah and Darren who are always there and to all who have dreams, shattered or whole.

Lizard Reality

Indigo Dreams II

Ronnie Goodyer

To Hannah and Darren who are always there and to all who have dreams, shattered or whole.

Lizard Reality

Indigo Dreams II

Ronnie Goodyer

Published by bluechrome publishing 2004

2 4 6 8 10 9 7 5 3 1

First published in Great Britain in 2004 by
bluechrome publishing
An imprint of KMS Limited
PO Box 109,
Portishead, Bristol. BS20 7ZR
www.bluechrome.co.uk

All pictures from the pen of Ronnie Goodyer

ISBN   0 954 3796-8-3

About The Author

Ronnie Goodyer is a multi-published and award-winning
poet, poetry judge, editor and artist who has appeared in
magazines such as Aireings, Aesthetica, Black Mountain
Review, Coffee House Poetry, Dial 174, Eclipse, Envoi, iota,
Konfluence, Moonstone, Poetry Cornwall, Poetry Monthly,
Poetry Nottingham International, Purple Patch, Poet Tree,
Solo Survivors, Reach, The Coffee House and The Journal.
He has been included in numerous anthologies, among those
being Dancing Through The Pain and Off The Wall for
MIND, Pulling Funny Faces at the Dog for NSPCC, Flowers
on a Shoestring for ONE-TO-ONE children's charity and
Listening to the Birth of Crystals to aid deaf children.

Previous Collections

Within The Silence   ISBN 1-900824-17-5
Indigo Dreams   ISBN 0-9543796-2-4
and as editor
bluechrome anthology 2004   ISBN 0-95437967-5
boho women peeling oranges ISBN 1-904781-05-5
A Sporting Chance   ISBN 1-904781-08-X

Thanks go to those who have been friends through a really traumatic period, particularly Andy and Natalie Kevin Bailey Gloria and David Brown Eileen Carney Hulme Anthony Delgrado 'Brutus' Chris Gifford 'Radar' Les Merton Ruth Musker 'Windy' Trish O'Brien Mark Rubra 'Cheffy' Vicky Stevens and Peter Tomlinson 'Wilf'
and in final memory of two great mates who died this year, Woof and Pat.

contents

Poem I Had To Write

Of course we'll meet again:
Sometime when the walk seems empty;
when the track through the wheat field
resounds with a towering sense of loss;
when the young cattle have no need to stir
and the vast meadow seems pointless,
devoid of play, sticks on the ground remain
to decay, not transform to an essential
possession to be carried and guarded;
when surplus food isn't stared at longingly
and mealtimes are enjoyed in peace.
Such sad peace.
When the rippling waves are quiet,
not the fearful breakers that can cover
unwary ears, sting unsuspecting eyes;
when the summer ponds are clear,
not muddied through too-eager paws;
when the house is quiet to strangers calls,
the post unhindered and unmolested,
the mundane is just that, not raised
by excitement or the sheer joy of life;
when the house doesn't smell peculiar
after walks in the rain and the drying
towel remains unused on its door hook;
when the path through the village fields -
where Lizard meadows tumble to the sea
and Falmouth gazes back from the bay -

is too painful for the burden of my eyes
and now untroubled by my footsteps;
when reason is abandoned for emotion,
sleep takes far too long to come
and dreams are all of a troubled kind.
Of course we'll meet again:
You're there at every turn.

For Skippy.

A View From Here

"a watercolour microcosm of Kernow...."

A View From Here

Ghosts at Gunwalloe

Here, the spectre of a rolling thunder-cloud
fights a south-westerly crosswind
right on the grassed crest of Gunwalloe.
The coarse rush waves in the sand
alive with footprints of a million ancestors,
carrying the catch, hauling the boats,
life telling in the burden of their eyes.

I meet the cry of the tossed buzzard
arcing to a speck by the tiny church,
a watercolour microcosm of Kernow.
Sun traces rays behind the black sky
which wrap my thoughts in sparkling ribbons,
healing and refreshing, waiting to be lifted
by the wings of each gust from the downs.

The rock formations are shadows of soldiers
streaked with the sweat of sacrifice,
returning here to their secret dreams,
praying for rebirth in the storm's windsong.
Rooks return to the Goonhilly heath
as the rain sways in bending light,
refreshing the sea, clearing the air.

I can hear the voices of thanksgiving
echo between the breakers and the shore,
as, in the lea, orange lights the glow of home.
I keep the promise to all who walked here,
all who gave me this life and this hope,
as I witness the last sigh of spring
and open my heart to the birth of summer.

On Gwynver Beach

Winter winds blast the breakers five lines deep
and whip the top foam to spiral deaths. She is
striding determinedly ahead to nowhere in particular
but drawn to the black cliffs, to the golden mist
trailing from the sun, as rain and night's early clouds
circle and loom, highlighting the contrasts of colour.

Her bobbled hat is alive, her footprints so small
next to mine, her tread so light. The vulnerability
of her busy little frame accentuated by her shadow
falling long on the sparkling sand behind her,
taller now than she'll be when childhood is over.

Men Scryfa

From sacred Boskednan Circle
waist-high green to the stone.
The granite pillar with long shadows
linking Celto-British to the present
for Ryalvran, the Royal Raven,
son of the Glorious Prince,
who saw death sweep from the west.
Men Scryfa, stone of writing,
the word outliving the sword.

By Crantock Beach

Beneath the sands and in another time,
Langarrow is buried;
Between Pentire Point's rocky headlands,
Langarrow is sleeping;
By the grassy plateau of Rushy Green,
Langarrow is resting.

Mysterious flat rock with woman and words,
who carved you?
'Mar not my face but let me be'
 'in this lone cavern by the sea'

'Let wild waves around me roar'
Langarrow is sleeping;
'kissing my lips for evermore'
Langarrow is resting;
Beneath the sands and in another time,
Langarrow is buried.

quotations from carving on rock
near Crantock Beach

Along Pork Hill

Like miniature islands on thirsty land,
white clouds skirted Cox Tor,
into the valley of pre-history farmers
who herded and reared with flint and chert tools.

At far skylined Brentor, St Michael de Rupe
silhouetted on the conical hill. On the slope
of Roos Tor geometric fields absorbed colour
with the sleeping granite landmarks unmoved.

Rooks, as doom's harbingers, disappeared high
over Great Staple Tor, this majesty holding
amphitheatre in square construction, frozen
and thawed to a thousand mind-shapes.

For some, long fingers point out caves
and for others, royal-ascent statuettes.
Clitter lies in profusion by the dewpond
falling short of the pony horizon, gathered

to slake thirst or hold herd-structure council.
This is where ancestors left their mark
and the Merrivale stones retain their secrets,
perhaps to be revealed on some new tomorrow.

Heart Of Stone

Guardian of stone,
You stand alone,
Remembering a dark-eyed people
Who understood the language of the land.

Heart of stone,
Beating forever
In synchronicity with earth and stars,
Fire waiting to awaken the dream.

Cast in stone,
Charged with emotion,
You touch and remember down the years.
The earth has a long, long memory
With a heart of stone.

Borne Beneath This Sun

When the wind doesn't blow the Coverack coastline
and the tide that soaks the shingle doesn't rise;
then we'll hide in the hills beneath the harbour,
where I'll lie beneath the laughter in your eyes.

When the rain drives the sun from sands at Kennack
and the ships that sail the Helford slip away;
then we'll hide in the skyline of the evening,
where we'll lie until the breaking of the day.

Porthallow feels the seasons through its breezes
and Porthoustock feels the seasons through its stones;
Godrevy feels the winds that brush the reed-beds,
where the isolation echoes through your bones.

You cannot tell the buzzards to stop wheeling
and you cannot tell the primrose not to flower;
you cannot tell the water to flow gently,
where its waves rise up and crash down with their power.

When the Gillan cliffs grow crazy with gulls' calling
and the gabbro rock reveals just where we've gone;
then we'll walk the ancient tracks to timeless borders,
where we're grateful to be borne beneath this sun.

This June

This June, with the shadows so black
and welcoming under the still gorse
and leaning trees, we walked the hill
to Carn Barges, paused to rest and
sit breathless together on the slope.

The sun had melted the green under
foot, so it slid to the rocks at Carn Scathe,
diffusing to a silver sea, blue only visible
against the nearest cliffs, still and solid.
Stretched by the flowered sea-pinks, the

lighthouse of Tater-Du was painted oils
in the watercolour view. We picnicked
on the wild cliffs of Porthcurno, the bees
droning like a far motorway and the sweet
smell of fresh hay from a hidden farm.

Upward again to Boscowan Point's summit,
where our laughter broke the silence and fell
to the suntrap coves of Paynter and St Loy,
held in the sub-tropical leaves and fronds.
This day, this June, like no other before it.

The Tractor With Green Hair

For years the Lizard winds were tamed,
infamous rain ignored, rare snows bridled.
The sheds collapsed, nature had reclaimed

the brick when pregnant fields became barren
and, unsustainable, human life had to cease.
OK, he told his ancestors, sorry, I'm beaten.

Abandoned in a wilderness meadow, visible now
and in cruel witness, an ageing tractor, rust
a vantage point for seeds established for years,

a natural burial mound by the rodents playpen,
by the barn with wet feet, by the decay carpeting all
- the tractor with green hair.

Princetown Picture

South Hessary, the Lookout Tor,
no longer seeking the Napoleonic invaders
but settled in a granite guard,
passing weather and tales with neighbours
Hart, Great Mis, Walkham and its northern namesake.

The dry dirt track winds through the moor, passing
Nun's Cross, an ancient waymark of foot patrols
from Buckfastleigh to Buckland Abbey, noting
the confirmation *Crux Siwardi:Bocland.*and
seeking the spire of St Michael and All Angels.

The painted horse-drawn carriages long gone,
no longer following the agricultural seasons
but distant with the passing of gypsy lore.
The hazel is still cut with gypsy craft here
and quartered sticks drawn by knives to flower shapes.

Again in the high heat of July summer, mother
and foal, in pastoral disregard, investigate the old track-way,
their shortened shadows accentuating the watching sun,
burning to the cloud-chasing hills, racing each reflection
and disturbing sheep, sleeping in two's behind granite.

The stallion, white and proud, stands under the oak,
happy and warm in this season's gift, gentle
until the Dartmoor mists break from a collapsing sky
to remind all that this last great wilderness is both
a beautiful friend and a fearsome enemy.

To Avalon

Emerging from Camlann's swirling morning mists
with his blood forming red pools on earth, the angels
under starlight now retreated to the waiting blackness,
King Arthur, magnificent in approaching death,
entrusted Bedivere to carry out his final task, to
give his sword, its life's work and duty completed,
its resting place below the waters of Dozmary Pool.

As I passed it over, I was aware of the life in the gold
and silver, the spirit it gave, almost god-like, a power
of possession so powerful, I was invisible, immaculate.
Bedivere rode to Bodmin Moor, with rainbow trails
emitting from the sword Excalibur, held to his chest
but fastened with sparkling gossamer to his heart.

Excalibur! To say the name was holy, to touch
a privilege of life taken to the cusp of legend.
Our horses nostrils flared breath to the crisp air
by the waiting brown-green reeds at the pool's edge.
The rushes and time-worn wooden stakes walked
unseen steps deeper into brackish water, wind-blown
to sparkle indigo and draw you to its very heart.

Above, a wheeling buzzard screamed at the day,
something was stirring, something very special
was happening that day. Fathomless and isolated,
Dozmary Pool was ready to receive, hold and protect.
Twice Excalibur was drawn and held to the light,
twice Bedivere could not release, his mind full of
voices, the sword telling him days of battles, magic
and the secrets of the past that he wished to know.

Excalibur could make the wise-ones pass the myths
into reality, the ancient stones speak of the days
of the old ones. He believed that to be pierced
by the sword would show him all he wished to know,
the things he could never, should never see.
Holding aloft for the final time, its mighty glare
alive and burning holes in his eyes, Bedivere threw.

Excalibur twisted as if under its own control, hovered,
then began its downward spiral of light to the pool.
One more secret was left…………….. one more.
As the clouds reflected on the wind and waves,
changes occurred. Time was in slow-motion now,
heartbeats slow and steady; people could not move.
Transfixed, the sword cut through solid air, as if removing
the mystery and wizardry that once ruled by Tintagel,
stripping the earth of all but the mundane, the logical.

Dozmary's waters looked solid, a thin plate reflecting
all, glowing with colours seen only in dreams. Dreams
that held coloured rain in tiny hands for the thirsty to drink;
dreams that protected the fragile egg so the gentlest dragon
could emerge and protect with gratitude; dreams that saw
herds of white unicorn turn to clouds above our heads.
Dreams that saw the waters part and a white-sleeved
arm appear, grasp Excalibur and slowly take beneath.

Gone. We heard the wind once again, looked in vain
for the dragon but he was gone. We were vulnerable.
Mortally wounded, looking frail, Arthur stood at the edge.
The burden clear in his eyes, he was ready for the trip.
We placed him on the barge hewn from English oak,
kissed him for the final time and watched him drift.
Again the mist fell. We heard a song, somewhere,
fading to the distance. Our King had gone to rest.
To Avalon.

Perpetual Time

Perpetual time on a black-sky evening,
entombed in dark and safely sealed;
church-bell chimes dissect the stillness,
while my ancestors' roam the field.

Perpetual time and the buzzards are diving,
village resounds to the mariners' cry;
Manacle Rocks the scourge of the vessels,
now home in the churchyard, anchored for life.

Perpetual time in a Cornwall August,
fire from the forges roaring aloud;
here on Lizard's tumbling landscape,
the ghost of An Gof is standing proud.

Perpetual time and crammed in the box-pews,
men of the village and wives of the men;
called to pray through copse and clearing,
holiday Tennyson wielding the pen.

Perpetual time on a landscape evening,
ancient track-ways are leading the eye
through myths and mists and vibrant tomorrows,
blending as one under Cornwall sky.

July Saturday, Coverack

'The tide'll be right up in an hour or so.'
I broke the news to the family, just
arrived and setting up home on the flat
sand by the rock wall. Not pleased.
What the hell do they do? They asked.

'Come back around four' I suggested,
' the beach will be back, cleansed by
the retreating sea, sparkling as it dries
to powder-sand. The rock-pools will be
new, full of life and the sand-bar warm.

.

There'll be some activity in the harbour,
with the second trip by a few small boats,
all aiming for the point you see out there,
towards the Falmouth headland. And the
sun will light up Lowland Point with about
fifteen colours to frame the bay.'

'We just want to play football' they said.
So I showed them the best bit, where
the chip shop wafted gently to the pub
and disused capstans could be goalposts.

Kynance

It was quite a walk we had, you and I;
botany with John Ray, medicine with
Prince Albert and the glorious light that
put your footprints so small, your shadow
even smaller.

This was a place to breathe.

We rushed to Tennyson's waves and in
dog valley, the *ki-nans,* made love in the
cave on holy serpentine, with the Devil's
Bellows roaring us to climax and the suction
of the tide pulling us, in our throes, to the sea.

Naked movie-stars at the water's edge, we posed,
ran to take the south valley path, dressed, and in
laughter, returned to the brown shining cliff,
puffing and smiling, wet and deliberate.
We paused; and then we shouted its glory.
Kynance.

Trencrom Hill

You couldn't make it to Trencrom Hill in spring.
Instead you set your easel by the Old Carn
and caught the sliver of darkening sea by its
western slope, the orange that held shadow
circles in its enveloping petals and the soft
azure blue of a hypnotic and permanent sky.

That winter you were near its base again,
seeing the hill as a misted grey, five layers
of background deep, with indistinct outline.
Your focus was the golden glint on bare willow,
framing the rectangular bottom edge, leading
the eye perfectly to the backward-leaning
green-brown lines of the field. Cornish hedges
appeared as thin black lines separating four
meadows of four greens, the granite farm
hiding by a stark winter copse. Captured on
canvass now, this landscape view across
Trevethoe Barton to Trencrom's misty heights.

On the next day of bright winter, you were
persuaded to climb with me. I led you through
the bracken to the holy well, secure, inspiring
and then upward to the stone-pillared gateway.
On smooth rounded boulders, we sat to watch
the birth of clouds and felt the energy flow from
St Michael's Mount, through Trencrom and out
towards Ireland. This was not a place to paint.
It was a place to breathe. A good place to breathe.
You asked me to write the day onto a page. I agreed
- but only after the day's scents had started to drift
and winter sunset slowly darkened into familiar night.

Over My Shoulder

"a daughter formed inside her
and Kurani Village frowned"

Over My Shoulder

Gosford Green, Back Then

Phillip, with his University of Warwick politics,
so free from responsibility that he could live
for his ideals and have a solution to the world's
ills. Perfection often came from tyrants, he
told us. Never pre-judge just from what we
read in westernised sanitised history. Be the
Bolivian peasant, the worker building the
enclosures that would eventually bar him.

Becky's tongue would lightly run between the
gummed edges and squeeze together the two
papers. She would fill this with Virginia on the
laminate of her study-book and conversation
would continue but all eyes would follow her
fingers; rubbing brown-black resin along the
length, then lifting and folding, the tongue
glistening again to finally seal; one end twisted,
held and shook. Only then would we look up.

Siobhan would tell us that the protest singers
were just fake, singing of oppression and poverty
while lining their pockets, soaking up gullible
and impressionable fools, like Phillip, like me.
Don't buy the mock anger, read The Grapes
Of Wrath then decide or remain indolent.
But there's entertainment and beauty in
compassion too, we'd argue. And it wasn't
all protest. It was love and awareness too
and *Suzanne* had changed our concept of
what could be performed as music and the
Gates Of Eden could even change lives.

All around, just by the road, the solicitors'
offices threatened, awaiting referrals from
neatly positioned estate agents. The smoke
was free for us and held in our lungs until
released to discolour the clouds, lazily-hanging
perfume, the taste exquisite, unmistakable.
Becky asked us to explain just what was so
great about a poet who permanently begged
money, who stole suits and pissed the bed.
It was the perfect time to answer.
The green's metal railings successfully held
the world at bay, the street sounds diminished,
the bird-song enhanced. The girls heard the
music and held each other in dance. We just
lay in the sun, watched their dancing legs,
creased hems and flowered pants as they
revolved above us, happy in the union. Four
figures in a perpetual summer, Pinot Grigiot
on the grass, the scene panning higher until
merging into trees contained within an oval
of green, an oasis in the heart of the city.

A Time To Be Alive With Sunshine

A time to be alive with sunshine.
We'd all changed to Human Be-ins
and Grace Slick was very young looking.
We saw and acted out White Rabbit
and hunger took us to Digger meals,
free for all. At the Panhandle,
there was plenty of work and friends.
Mr Cohen sold Orange Sunshine,
Blue Barrels and White Lightning,
all legal, pre-October '66.

A time to be alive with sunshine.
We penetrated the open door
of Seven-ten Ashbury, where
the Grateful Dead lived with lovers,
including the various street-strangers.
We walked the pavement with Mountain Girl
and she carried her baby Sunshine.
Along the way we bought them presents,
green and scarlet bonnets, one-size, one-piece.
Mountain gave them away pretty soon.
The Charlatons came into town
as did Janis with her Big Brother.
We went out with assorted Peter Pans
to Petalumo Mansion, just curious.
Psychics, magicians and non-politics.

We both fell for the whole damn thing -
breathing and jumping and Yippie Reuben!
Still, we sang in some colourful choirs,
and agreed it was a good time to be alive.
A time to be alive with sunshine.

Hannah's Day
(13th December, 1988)

The heart raced
and the legs raced
and the schoolbag was dropped on the drive;
the clothes worn before were left on the floor
and she splashed in the bath before five.

The towel dried
and the child dried
and her brother cleaned up all the mess;
clean undies and socks, a choice of two frocks
then an angel in party-blue dress.

The blinds pulled
and the hair pulled
and the brown tresses teased into shape;
A wrinkle of nose as mum tied her bows
and there's only one hour to wait.

The bell rang
and the noise rang
and the children all played in the hall;
a mention of food, a scramble ensued
with some tears as one fell in the maul.

A child tore,
another tore
but the present lay hidden inside;
until Hannah ripped the last little bit
and she picked up the sweets as her prize

Music played
and children played
and some of them blew up balloons;
Kathy and Kara tried on mascara
while quiet ones just watched cartoons.

A shout - 'here!',
two more shouts - 'here!',
as they teased in a loud blind-man's-buff;
they dodged from the palms and two flailing arms
but a few found it all a bit rough.

The time went
and the cars went
and then all of the thank-you's were said;
Happy and weepy, Hannah was sleepy
so was carried by daddy to bed.

Writin' in Greece

Willin' the words,
marooned in my home;
choosin' the booze
for yogurt an' houmus.

Dylans' for verse,
a tune and a poem;
music an' muse
with Robert and Thomas.

Marianne, (and hazy jane) Paxos, summer

The view above the mist caught the beauty in her lie;
the view above reality, captured in her eye.
Flesh in heated hedgerows and warmth in time
together;
summer's season solely and time beyond the weather.

Shadows in the canyon in the land of her life's dream;
shadows on the mountain, where we made our own life's scheme.
Rain of powdered nature lightened steps on solid air;
footfalls crawled us higher till we reached the final stair.

Once when we were very young, we denied all reasons.
Once when we were very old, we defied all seasons.
Syrtaki sounding solely as we ran to catch our breath,
in that land of living cocktail, too high to fall to death.

Lantern days and crumpled clothes, stained red with cherry blood;
gloves of glowing amber in a night of sandalwood.
Sharing time with Hazy Jane and rhymes where minds can keep it;
back on sand with Marianne, and dawn drawn back in secret.

To Mandy, Unaware.

Your red hair suggests movement —
dangerous like a fire -
but you lie so still.

I'm saddened by the graph
showing your life in a line,
oblivious of all that I know.

You're blissfully unaware now,
monitored and nil-by-mouth.
I need to walk into shouting cars,

talk to you on some corner,
wait for you by the burdened trees.
A cry from the cemetery

resonates to your bedside
where you lie in a pre-dawn shadow
and moistened closed eyes show

your red hair suggests movement
but you lie so still.
So very still.

The Counsellor Helped (recurring)

The counsellor helped her aggression
by saying it was natural but she
should channel it the right way.

The counsellor helped her depression
by explaining which deep prejudices
had removed her natural aggression.

The Duck Of Nightfall

'Sally isn't good, Sally is bad,
Sally's got things that make her so sad.'
A lullaby of thirteen, going on fifty.

She had this pattern on her bedroom ceiling
which on windy nights formed a bobbing duck's head.
She used to stare at this until rocked gently
out of focus. Sally felt really safe with
her Duck of Nightfall. She was tormented
as a gnarled olive tree, electric light a
yellow explosion. But she'd got the shadow.
As comforting as biting her pillow.
As comforting as her cold bicycle shed.
As comforting as footsteps on the stairs.

Strange how the morning seemed so normal;
those tubular steel breakfast smells, the
newspaper rustle, even the 'see you later'
didn't appear as a threat, not as ominous.
A flick of brown hair and the click of the gate.
Oh - the click of that proprietary gate!
Solid as a rock and onto Freedom Road.
Holding hands with her friend and between raindrops,
Sally is dancing! Between the council privet
and the kerb, on a coat of thin air that blows
just for her. Last night's tears and fears?
Behind the gate! Happy times? On Freedom Road!
Childhood dreams? Riding with the duck of nightfall.....

The rain was beating heavily on the shelter.
Dark grey shoulders appeared on light grey raincoats.
Sally and a friend on a Saturday,
an approaching bus and a ticket to ride.

Trading

It was too hot again in Goa and I'd
left friends basking in kaftans and
nothing to walk along dust to the
shaded old town. A man was sitting
on the concrete, three newspapers
spread flat on the ground in front of
him, each paper seething with black
flies, some four deep fighting for position.
I was wondering why the hell he didn't
do something, until an elder approached.
She shouted, he shouted back, I watched.
He smashed his fist into the throng of flies,
then slowly lifted back each newspaper,
covering again when the woman had seen.
Under each one was brown-red meat
veined with grey fat, lying on the dirt.
They struck a deal. He fought off the
settling flies, wrapped the meat in the
newspaper, then took a handful of coins.

I went back to the beach to my friends.
Joss was singing Tim Hardin, 'If I Were
A Carpenter' and ten or so were sharing
a smoke. I waited to sing Leonard Cohen
- 'The Butcher.'

Stalker

You dismissed my friendly look
with an 'in another lifetime mate'
glare.

My brown eyes, believe me,
if that's what it takes, I'll be
there.

Eleven Lives Ago

I still have it,
the special gift you gave me when we
first met, eleven lives ago.

Here, in my new existence, I've finally
found you and can repay you at last
after all these lives.

In this world, though,
you don't recognise me
as you tell me what was beautiful
eleven lives before.

It means nothing now
in your loveless world
and perhaps I must wait eleven lives again
to return what I have.

Her Poem

There was silk
and sex,
then noise;
louder at first
than after.

Days later
she smiled,
as if she knew
I saw inside her poem
like no-one had
before.

Maria's on a Country Train

Maria's on a country train
in mainland Greece in summertime
Cicadas sing their Greek refrain
by countless trees and countless vines

In mainland Greece in summertime
platforms shimmering with the heat,
by countless trees and countless vines
her book left open on her seat.

Platforms shimmering with the heat,
while dreams invade her sleepy mind.
Her book left open on her seat,
white houses pass, all boxed in line.

While dreams invade her sleepy mind
with another hour to endure,
white houses pass, all boxed in line,
I wait in Athens as before.

With another hour to endure
she'll have completed journeyed miles.
I wait in Athens as before
with growing love and hidden smiles.

She'll have completed journeyed miles
cicadas sing their Greek refrain.
With growing love and hidden smiles,
Maria's on a country train.

Fox Dreams

I fox
at the corner
of all your dreams tonight.
You cannot harm me in your mind,
so safe

until
morning finds you
and once more I'm fur-bait
in your lame excuse for pleasure,
so sad.

But then
in sleep again,
I'm in your dreams' nightmares,
unsettling you with terror's bark.
So loud.

Beyond Ginnungagap

She's crossed over, floating in last night's void.
I was with her,
between fog
and fire,
now
proof
to all
she receives
her life's welcome -
after Antioch, her birth of Heaven.

In Umbrella Heaven

Memories of the Umbrella Club
in the midlands, where people
would just stand up from their
table, hold onto their beer and
recite their piece. My pal sang
My Back Pages by the other Dylan
and I thought that would cap the
night (free beer for the winning table)
but some guy stood up and read
Especially When The October Wind (it was June),
(emkcuf!) and we all felt the autumnal
spells, the spider-tongued and the loud
hill of Wales. The following weeks were
littered with band-wagonners, like me,
some with mock accents for the hywl.
Poetry could sing.
Poetry would sing forever.
Me? I just sang in my chains like the sea.

Cave Visit

The first cave was cool, all meanings,
inhabited for hundreds of years,
the walls white with cloth divisions
and candles to light various shrines.

Valley walls have a few homes left.
Like sea-birds on Atlantic cliff-faces,
these people planned for generations ahead
in the harsh world of the desert's dovecote.

The middle caves smelled of spices
and were dominated by great slabs of meat,
coated black and hanging on fearsome hooks,
linking directly back to the lost centuries.

You weren't much taken by the child,
looking to us ill beyond belief and wrapped
in layer on layer of blankets, with just
a tiny pair of indigo eyes visible in the blankness.

On the sand too hot to walk barefoot,
we were waved farewell by the man,
black-suited, black-hatted and gloved,
no trace of sweat, no trace of smile.

The Ballad Of Amina Lawal

The African sun is shining on
the bars that guard the prison,
as Amina Lawal counts the hours
and days upon this earth.
Remembering her search for love
and meeting with a stranger,
she signed her own death warrant
while she was giving birth.

The youngest child of thirteen she
fought hard for her survival
and married by family order
when she was just fourteen.
Twelve years stress and happiness
dissolved when she was subject
to the ending of her wedding,
the ending of her dreams.

The opening of another love
and joined in sexual union,
a daughter formed inside her and
Kurani Village frowned.
Her man denied all knowledge
and the courts believed his story,
leaving her to face the future
and stones upon the ground.

Sharia law is ruling with
floggings and amputations,
interpreting the Koran in the
harsh traditional way.
Adultery is proven now,
confirmed by new-born daughter
so she weans her out of wedlock,
waits for her final day

Twelve states out of nineteen states
in northernmost Nigeria
adopt the strict Sharia code
and she will soon be dead.
Like Taliban in Afghanistan,
she's condemned to death by stoning;
buried in earth up to her neck
then rocks rain on her head

The African sun is shining on
the bars that guard the prison,
as Amina Lawal counts the hours
and days upon this earth.
She found her love and found her child
and found a world uncaring,
ignoring pleas for leniency,
ignoring human worth.

*Written when Amina Lawal, found guilty of adultery, was sentenced in
2002 to be buried up to her neck and stoned to death. Given time to
wean her daughter Wasila, she was scheduled to be executed sometime
after January 2004. This has since been rescinded.*

Starkweather

Just 'cos people are different an' all
that doesn't mean y' can't TALK to 'em,
or listen 'n that. That's no hard thing.

Starkweather at nineteen,
James Dean with Caril Ann,
garbage man with a bow-legged girlfriend.
Unprepossessing, red hair and a rifle.

Shot the parents, choked the child.
Three corpses and an open door.
In the wind, seven days, seven bodies,
Lincoln, Nebraska to Douglas, Wyoming.

Dead were all god-damned sons-of-bitches,
All-seeing, all-hating, all the power
that persecution brings, welled up in
the selfishness of the shotgun.

Starkweather at twenty,
ten notches and relief from the fire,
practised the meanness in the world,
no place with people he knowed,
snapped his head back, smiling.

Between Blinking

"between light
and dark sand
white foam"

Between Blinking

life

seventh birthday
orange-juice on party dress
small bites in the cake

her first poem
paper balls on the carpet
tears by the ink spot

telephone mother
it now takes eleven rings
before she replies

news of a death
silence in the garden
a crushed rose

flowers in metal vase
fresh petals blow on granite
and brush your name

fiftieth anniversary
new buds on the tree-stump

Sea Sex

between light
and dark sand
white foam

Watching The Bait Digger, Long Rock.

Three bands of sepia morning;
a top band with faint wisps of cloud;
 a centre band with flickering sea-silver;
a bottom band with the four-inch high
black frame of a man, stooping and
digging with a four-pronged fork,
leaving black castles in his wake.

Turning Away

twelve year old working
sex in a Bangkok side-street
sun is shining

therapist talking
empathy clouding the mind
the rapist talking

with the counsellor
burden leaking from her eyes
five minutes left

Across the Greens

Across the greens and orange-golds
you would lead and I would follow;
Boswen's Common's footprint tracks,
to the ridge of far Bosullow.

Green Burrow

One lone thorn tree
naked by the wind
and the one-chimney sky;
Green Burrow tin mine,
lost in time.

Cornwall Glimpses

stroking the church
sprouting from the lichen wall
foxgloves at Zennor

trodden green pathway
bluebells painting orange gorse
Madron Carn springtime

indigo water
the River Hayle at St Erth
still by moving reeds

mock snow in sunshine
moor grass in cotton flower
Chykembro Common

St Keverne square
war memorial's shadow
cloaks the pensioner

Lizard serpentine
battered by black waves
one pink flower

nature

by the sign
please do not feed the ponies
a foal waits for food

open countryside
sheep-wool blowing in barbed wire

two honey bees
dance for each other
showing the way

frosty spring morning
broken foil on milk bottle
bird flying away

caterpillar crawls
from living leaf
to child's finger

moorland pony
reveals its winter journey
hoofprints in frost

fresh grass bends heavy
with birthing seed

dew shining in pools
on velvet-mossed bark
thirsty lizard drinks

wind blows meadow grass
dandelion seed trapped
in the spider's web

In Coronation Park, Helston

The silence of a passing spring,
concrete yielding to instant water
on the other side. On the other side.

We sit in wood-borne tranquillity,
chilled wine and an occasional word.
Waiting. Listening. Ready for summer.

Christmas

atheist lady
under pagan mistletoe
kissing the vicar

Regressive Aggressive

High on crack and crime he kicked
his mother's stomach. Refusing to
prosecute, she explained how he
used to do that in the womb and
how she forgave him then, too.

one Sunday

late into church
footsteps echoing
like god's thunder

vicar in pulpit
man checks his watch
opening time

cold conversation
clouds of breathe
hide your words

crystal in sun
two cats in the glow
furred rainbows

Lifting At The Edges

" I was trying to stroke heartache,
hold heartbreak and there's Dog
having the time of his life..."

Lifting at the Edges

Trying to be a Lonesome Poet, with Dog

Dog was standing in the rock pool. I was trying
to have this really bad day but had to help him
check for crabs and stuff. It delayed the morose
melancholy I was seeking. He ran off toward the
harbour where the boats rocked in the bay. I just
acknowledged the water-sky beauty for others as
I dived into my tunnel of depression. I was seeing
my life in the sadness of empty rooms and doorways,
then Dog dropped his ball at my feet. I hurled it,
he ran for it caught it, jumped for it, wagged his
non-sympathetic tail at everyone. I was trying to
stroke heartache, hold heartbreak and there's
Dog, having the time of his life. I moved on to
icy miles, silent telephones, utter rejection. This
was better. Dog hounded some family for a piece
of their picnic as I was well into broken love, new
love, no love; letters in holding-hands texture, lost,
lonely times. Then Dog appeared, chewing a crust.
Then a kid came up carrying his ball. Bloody hell.

I followed the sound of a far-off ship, trying to see
where it was from. As if I cared. From the harbour
to the shop-fronts, still looking down at the scarred
pavement. Over the sea, dusk was glowing neon.
I ignored it. Three friends whistled Dog to the pub.
I sat with the stripped feelings, canned laughter,
choking on tomorrow's sad pasta. The angst was
gaining momentum but I had to call into the pub to
collect Dog, maybe have five or six beers of remorse.
The friends were settled for a few hours, so I had
to try to be jolly for longer than expected. Dog was
by the music-machine, helping Jan choose a tune.
A sad one, I hoped.

Working at Boots

Siobhan worked at Boots
and she smelled of my future.
I spent hours looking but not
looking, at the albums. You
see, this was helpful Boots
where the assistants came
to your side to help – and
sometimes that was Siobhan.

She saw me through Trout
Mask Replica, discussed
the poetry of addict Tim Hardin,
shared Dylan's rock transition,
assured me Forever Changes.
She proved McCartney was
dead, pointed to the faces
hidden in the shadowed tree.

But she was three years
older than me at the age
where it really mattered.
And she left Boots without
telling me she was going.
So I questioned her sincerity
and realised Weasels Ripped
My Flesh was just a noise.

I moved on to Tom Rush
melodies, was soothed by
Joni Mitchell, with Ravi
Shankar filling my nights
with a Song From The Hills.
This is what I'd been after,
this was true, was the real me.
New-girl Anna really knew her stuff.

Under A Summer-Blue Sky

Mr Grey walked through
the grey door to his grey office today
met all the poets and painters today
no time for rhyme or for colour today
met all the actors and turned them away
no time for mime or for mummer today
told all the writers what they had to say
diction in fiction is friction today

but he licks his lips at a pile of bricks
talent has come when a light is switched on
and he nods his head at an unmade bed
real art for now – a formaldehyde cow
a game of two halves a fame of two calves
(we don't know if this is taking the piss)
then he goes home where he's bored to the bone
under a summer-blue sky.

Naked Lunch

So just what is it you do again?
You let people eat from your navel?
You don't want a table-dancer's fame –
as you'd much rather be the table.

Do you worry, lying nakedly,
so completely devoid of your clothes,
that perhaps a bean or errant pea
may choose adventure within your nose?

And what do the diners' say or think
as you're wearing their salad dressing?
That maybe the radish won't grow limp,
or that your croutons need caressing?

Do you, at night, when deep in slumber,
ever dream of a rogue cucumber?

Off on one (four)

Powerful Punctuation

My best friend Paul's beautiful sister.
My best friend – Paul's beautiful sister.

Rendezvous

I said
meet me in the
short stay car park. She said
yes, okay, but I can't stay long.
Vroom vroom.

Tempered Love

If only
she'd keep
her hair on
she'd be someone
I'd heap
my care on.

Insecticide Ditty

Oh, I think I must wander to purchase again
some dichlorodiphenyltrichloroethane.
Then insects will get a wet present from me,
the great colourless, odourless D…………..DT

Portrait of the Poet as a Sad Git

Suzanne was taking me down
to her place by the river when
my friends came in for a beer.

'Ugh jeez…….Leonard Cohen,
deep despair…..show me where
the lemmings are gathering…yuk.'

And there was me, singing along,
closing eyes, really enjoying it.
Sad git.

Phone Fatale

If a man
says rude things
to a woman
he is liable to get arrested.

If a woman
says rude things
to a man
it'll cost around a pound a minute. Peak.

Just A Few Non-haiku

'pool traffic warden
she's got a ticket to write
and she don't care

night shift worker
sleeping on the mezzanine
floor in the system

too much talking
too little happening
all words and no play

meaningful noise from
a pigeon above the clouds
- a high coo

Tetractys

Uncertainty

Is
the word
'waterworks'
just one word or
two words separated by a hydrant?

An Orphan Tetractys

'Who
was that
orphan I
saw you with last
night?' 'That was no orphan, that was my waif.'

The Demise of G.M. Crops and the Side Effects Caused by the New Solution

Nothing in the fields anymore
GM crops failed
Boarded up the countryside
Farmers all jailed
We know you're hungry
There's no food anywhere
So here's the solution
To show government cares
See the dogs in the park
So freely at play
Yes here's the solution
It's the canine way

EAT DOG FOOD

1.One or two side effects
   No cause for alarm
   Like if you're a postman
   You'll bite your own arm
2.You can't ride horses
   Not allowed on the saddle
   Your freestyle crawl will be
   A swift doggy-paddle
3.Going on holiday
   You'll have to remember
   You're not allowed on the beaches
   April through September
4.You'll become an integrator
   Of the social classes
   Because you'll greet everyone
   By sniffing their asses
5.You'll have to accept that
   Kissing will be different
   Now you'll smell of dog-breath
   Quite nasty on the whiff-front
 6.Men – if you want to be
   Big beefy hunks
   Spend a little more and buy
   Big meaty chunks
7.Girls – to be a supermodel
   You'll just never have a care
   Just eat like you always have –
   Absorb moisture from the air

So that's our proposal
We suggest you make notes
(And please, on Election Day,
 Don't piddle on the votes)

Lessons In Mind-Shaping

"all the while his head was soaring"

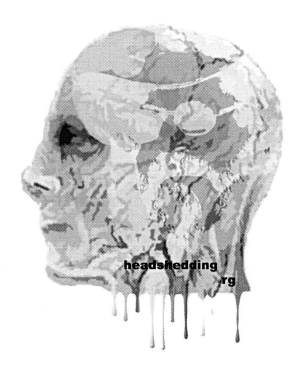

Lessons in Mind-shaping

My Father's Image

We used to sit on the edge, watch things
in celluloid, while father was upstairs
in the bathroom. He stood in front of
the mirror and stared. For hour upon hour.
He liked the way his appearance blurred
at the edges then dipped sharply back
into focus. He was careful not to deliberately
move his eyes, just allow spasms to control.
This way he could see his true self, he said.
And pretty soon the background would change
from pigment-blue to a universe of swirling
indigo with black stars, static black with
white stars. All the while his head was soaring,
feeling the freshest breezes from the purest
winds, entering his face and coursing with
his blood-oxygen, renewing, each trip a rebirth.
His skin like a stretched balloon, he had to
know just when to stop breathing new air
inside, stop before the explosion. This he
did by holding his breath until his face
disappeared behind white stars and began
to sway. Then he would snap shut his eyes,
causing him to lurch forward and steady
himself on the lip of the sink. Duly composed,
he'd return to us, sit on the edge, watch celluloid.

Jealous

Walking the strand of sand at Porth Chapple
I saw your arms prone on the greyer strip by
the sea, your hands clinging to a granite rock
recently slipped from the cormorant cliffs.

Where the sea lapped green by the shore,
your legs were astride a submerged mound
and thrusting, lubricating the streaming weed,
forming waves that rocked in uniform motion.

Your head was partially visible in the far blue
and your breasts would occasionally break surface,
nipples wet and proud, shadowing back in monolith
black, too far to touch. Back on the sand, people

emerged from the slipway and settled to watch
the breakers build in momentum as you climaxed,
your voice a siren in the high air, white foam
crashing to the cubist rocks framing the bay.

Family Business

I saw him who was head of his land
I saw her put her hand in his hand

I saw him treating people like dirt
I saw her just adjusting her skirt

I saw strangers dismissing the guard
I saw both of them staring real hard

I saw guests leave their table in haste
I saw both of them looking white-faced

I saw shadows that weren't there before
I saw both of them dead on the floor

I saw soldiers dispersing the crowd
and a son that was looking quite proud

Family House

It was much too big to be alone in.
The pine table sat eight, six along
the sides, one at each end. There
were so many cupboard doors and
drawers and two huge windows
looked from the kitchen over the
lawn to the goose and goat field
beyond. This was much too big
a view to look at alone.

Round the side of the house,
the old oak centred the second
lawn, the pond separated it from
the third. Pond. I made it from
that plastic-stuff guaranteed for
twenty years and left a lower side,
so it would flood to give that marsh-
garden with the plants and marginals
we loved in the wild.

Third lawn? Out the back by the
sit-in bay of the lounge, leading
off through a half-acre of mature
woodland, with seasoned mistletoe,
huge banks of rhododendron and
a giant honeysuckle. Oh, and the
stream that flowed when the trees
were bare. The road was someway
off, linking Abergavenny to the world.

Just now and again you could hear
the low rumble and shake of a lorry,
mainly though you heard the chiff-chaff
following you around, marking your
territory, chiff-chaffing at you till it near
drove you crazy. I let the potatoes just
run on. I blamed that lost weekend
when the four of us planted them,
covered in muck, messing about.

Hannah'd called earlier on, left
a bottle. 'Got you some Bulgarian
Cabernet Sauvignon dad. Only cheap.
Hope it's not too shitty!' That evening
I sat on the lawn, the second one,
and spurred on by the chiff-chaff,
wrote to a lot of people I knew.
Just something and nothing letters,
like you do when you're reflective.

Seemed to do a lot of staring then.
Found myself doing a lot of staring.

And when I went to the geese and
goats, I stooped on haunches to talk
to them. Felt good but so solitary.
Back on the lawn, I sat under the
tree and drank the wine. It wasn't
shitty at all, quite pleasant in fact.
Just not enough to drink alone.
Needed far more thought and comfort.

Painter Portrayal

Jewish refugee parents setting up
homes for the elderly, you in the
green-vinyl world of Room Three,
encountering the people set to inhabit
your universe; those with all hardships,
the wildly philosophical, the slightly
un
    hinged.

From Royal Academy schooling to
follow worthy ways, London studio
home to the homeless, the disillusioned.
You were respectfully asked to leave.
To Plymouth where they loved you, rolled
in the canvas of your world, invested in
the bohemia, devoted to the manifestations.

Cowboy Holiday Inns sheltering many
from the storms, handing back respect
and belief once again. Unsurprisingly
your first paintings in the 'Relativity',
the start of twenty, were of vagrants.
You made hollow eyes cry, reach-out.

Books and art left a legacy. The World
Imperial Library. A start-point for your
mind. Did you find the cause of obsessive
and fanatical behaviour? The reasons
behind belief systems? Love? Are the
answers concealed in your paintings?
Will we know where to look now you've gone?

Lenkiewicz 1941-2002

Just Dancing

Young and wanting, this feel of
fresh feelings; the yawn of the park
river just noticed; the glass shadow
of Wimpy; the terror of disco.

You smelled of the future from a
bottle from Boots. It stayed the scent
of romance through many liaisons;
it held nostalgia and that bloody
first-love pang. Came to nothing.

And when you were leaving six years
later, after being just friends, nothing more,
you stripped in the window so I could
see you one last time. You wrote to ask
if I'd seen you, did I take notice, get horny.

I'd got this letter I didn't send. Just asking
why it didn't work because my heart was
bleeding. I just wondered if maybe, after
snogging in the park and eating at Wimpys,
perhaps, one time, we'd danced too close?

A Glass For Woof

It was good to have conversation,
though he struggled for breath and strength.
We talked geology through Stella, shared the views
and he showed me the coves he knew, explored, fished.
He sent me off to where he'd like to go again, and I thanked
him with an image of the place, the change. Fighting cancer
took too much strength; adding diabetes was a sick joke.
It was good talking to Woof: About wine, stratiography,
words and wildlife, my cider pouring from the
three litre as the crack of the flip-top
and glug to the glass meant
he was OK, he was
still in there.

g
o
o
d
b
y
e
Woof
Tenth of May 1934 to Fourteenth of February 2004

Being Alone In The House

Being alone in the house, my legs were leaden
and the doors were stiff, reluctant to sway.

I sat in the barely recognisable room
as she entered, pushing the empty wheelchair.

'I still live here,' she justified, 'and when I'm mad
I push this against the wall. Wasn't always empty.'

And I remained, being alone in the house,
dragging from room to room, leaning against doors,

determining the source of the sounds – tubular steel,
metal on plaster, spinning wheels and tormented sighs.

Dream Chant For The New World

Too worn by the world
and the values of the Master,
there's a glow in the fields
where future ancestors are haunting me.

Can anyone else's eyes see
the monk on the road?
the stars in the hedge?
the spin of the planet?

God is in his heaven
and they're killing him again,
they're killing him again
and we're killing him again.

Power of the pyramids   (shine in the dream)
Illuminated citadel   (shine in the dream)
Circle of Stones   (shine in the dream)
Music of the mosque   (shine in the dream)

Exotic strangers please take me,
on the dirt by the stars, please take me,
by the shadow of the cross, please take me,
by England's myth of granite.

Blind me tonight   (and then to the dream)
give me your dark   (and then to the dream)
there are no weapons, exotic strangers,
for all the world is naked.

Now is the time to swim in the tears,
to hear on the waves
and to search for me in the soil.
(And then……..to the dream.)

Plants

Outside my bedroom window,
separating my vision from the
field to the sea, it's all pink and
white mallow. And as it shifts,
it's clearer than the clunk of my
door, the voice I ignore. Scary.

Underneath is cyclamen, fuchsia,
polyanthus, fern, roxella, buddleia.
And with the scent of honeysuckle,
I see the empty car park, see the
distant space you always warned
me about. I was too hasty.

I was rushing to see you.
And yet missing you again.
Just like I missed the plant
in the hedge. Love Lies Bleeding.

Retrospective

You said you wouldn't ring too often and
there was no need for me to keep ringing.

You were OK and I was glad because
mostly your calls went on forever with
stuff repeated at least twice, so I didn't ring.

When you fell on the floor in that cold kitchen,
with your around-neck alarm on the table by
the phone (always a place for pride, Ronnie,
you said), and you lay there for four days,

until a neighbour found you, well, I'm glad
it was in no way my fault. You said, with
the last few breaths of your speaking life,
there was no need to keep ringing.
So I didn't. I didn't ring.

Isolated Garden

From the kitchen's creaking,
all around the mind-pipers' mind
into the garden's sniff-and-see.
Sweet-flowing in pulp-berries,
in stinging pear and blighting weeds
green and stem.
A black-lined hole of wasted hours,
old echoes and Scream faces,
the summer scene and scents churn,
fly-days of fire wooden pretence,
the sparkling ash of resisted blame,
mockery fear isolation submission.

The dog sleeps...............
positioned back on grass, star-shaped
under looming trees with cartoon mouths,
yielding a cry magnified by tears
taken from the memory before summer
was a-goin'-out and laughter rang from
small shoes, from the whirl of the fairground
and rise of the merry-go-round.

A morning in the deep deep garden
from circles down down the night
and now standing soaking in vestments,
trodden dew and discarded juices poured
from the glow of heaven to dank glasses.
Someone shouts for burgundy, someone's
drunk on peat, confusing the mind-piper,
to allow flat talk and a walk over ground
to a half-bottle and a call from friends.

To small shoes, abandoned, in an empty fairground.

Poaching

When Paul told me he was a poacher,
I got this idea of the stalker, the moon,
and the search for quarry by trained eye.

So four of them went to the trout stream.
Just by the fall they dragged net curtain
across to bridge. While two held, the other
two went upstream, poured garden lime
into the water. Everything died. The trout
were gathered in the curtain, the lesser
creatures, the water snails, the beetles,
the essential elements of water life, just
disappeared somewhere. The lime poured
over the fall to dissipate eventually and, I
was reassured, 'this has no effect on the
taste of trout.' So that's OK then.

When Paul told me he was a poacher,
he ruined my image forever, naïve fool
that I was. Now I knew. Uncaring bastards.

Terza Rima Dreamer

Yes, I know I broke a promise
but I never intended to.
I just didn't know it would be like this,

your father questioning me about you
until I was scared to take a breath,
what about this and was that true

and your mother 'politing' me to death.
You check your balance on the net.
I check my change and then guess

whether I should call, or let
you sleep off a lunched Sunday,
not knowing the reply I'd get.

I think that my dream of 'one day'
was among my more optimistic schemes.
You're on a higher plane to where I play

and, sadly, different streets and different means
have combined to give me different dreams.

Emptiness

Here, words mean nothing.
Here, time is irrelevant.
Here, birds don't fly in the wind
or the vacuum embrace.
Here, is waiting for meaning,
opportunity and will.

I will leave the distinction of sorrow,
the complete pride of nothing.
(A sadness of possession remains most
clearly when you leave nothing behind.)

I Miss You

I miss you so much.
Broken-down love means so much.
A dream-time once told me
I need gold-faced meadows
to sing their sweet songs.
But I just miss you,
so much.

Sunday Afternoon

The tension in the air blunts
the peeping of the cloudy sun,
the swallow of tea echoing threat,
after the argument, during the silence.

Rehearsed dismissive glances
and mock enthusiasm in distractions,
a growing desire to share opinion
with any disinterested party.

An island of splendid isolation
with the party about to happen,
the voices which will regain normality
and the trivial item which will restore

the bond of utter love that exists
and allow tacit acceptance on this
Sunday afternoon of total boredom
and hogwash, rubbish TV.

For Morgan

As the four-mile wind
whipped the gorse and hazel,
it scooped airborne a wheeling flight,
a swarm of dying leaves.

As the sky-dance tumbled
these brown, coppered petals
in a fixed spiralling curve,
you jumped to catch, barking.

Now, they just settle on grass.
Now, I just carry on walking.

A Poem of Parting

Dancing just a little too close
and falling at night to the smell of
smoky Indian fabric across her knees,
this was always destined to the roller-ride
that excited, elated, plunged with uncertainty
through the unknown force; with love emblazoned
in a picnic of the wild, kissed by Dartmoor and washed
by the naked sea, the salty smell of the day, the salty taste
of the night's foraging. Sadness with the dolphin on the beach,
the flies in the eye-sockets blinding sight that to others remained
sharp and clear. Fresh as a Cornish lane after rain she was, a delicacy
that bowed the morning rose with dew, facing the pitted earth, not
rising to glow in its true colours. Deep in the iron-works of a lost
time, we stumbled in spirituality and legend, shared the sun
and the pools of leaf-mist held in ancient forests, listened
to stone-circles warning us of a frail future. Alas and
alas, against the tree, full of summer and green,
just alone together. She died then, dissolving
before my eyes into its roots, absorbed to
rise on another Spring when I was far
away. The tree stands somewhere
with other spirits in the wood,
while I explore landscapes
of clay and sand, with
roses waving to a
new morning,
their colours dulled in the watering of eyes, their smell of smoky Indian
fabric, unfading.

Single Again, (naturally)

rainbow angels		misplaced walkers
pumpkin jokers	and	displaced talkers
dappled minds		cosmic sliders
cowboy poets	and	pale-moon riders
shaven wizards		bobsleigh babies
gypsy leaders	and	trapeze ladies
immaculate fools		freestyle buskers
alcohol thinkers	and	firework hustlers
mountain painters		captive cruisers
afternoon lovers	and	beautiful losers

Look to the road - the sad clown's coming

Link arms again - the sad clown's coming!

A View From There

"there's a secret in the doorway
if you care to look......"

A View From There

Lizard Reality

The airfield war buildings have been re-painted
in parts and perfumed by wisteria, indoor plants
wild outside and a hinterland of Jerseys on runways,
quiet shadows on the control tower and here the
big horse, nuzzling for love and natural, Dolly,
cart-horse from Dublin, now free as the people
co-habiting with truths and backdrops.

Closet lives with the doors open or closed; the
community of unity or confinement. There's a
secret in the doorway if you care to look. But
sometimes it's easier to hear the silence, watch
the clouds scud from Kennack to the sea that,
whilst forever moving, never changes.

Clones

Babushka.
Russian Doll.
Nesting Doll.
Caesarean sections
and a poor, stripped,
bleeding original doll.

Clone-lines trail
barefoot blood.
'Look behind you child,
your mother is dead.'

'It doesn't matter –
I'm the same.'

'Then surely **you**
don't matter?'

She holds her
mother's carcass,
shouts 'Why? Why?'

as the lines chant
'is-it-my-turn-yet?'
and I wake up,
just missing the news,
the day's progress.

The Night-Dreams of Angels

2 a.m. in that half-sleep I entered
the night-dreams of angels and found
their despair so comforting. I learned
that this other world is riddled with
jealousy and greed. The purpose
of this world's violence, to gain control
and manipulate, to starve others and
gorge yourself, had solid reason, the
poorer places had the richer churches.
God was casting out too and developed
his hierarchy to serve and worship.
Omnipotent.
It was better to fuck than make love,
take rather than give and the time spent
on compassion better spent on gain,
developing the material. Fashion was
more important than ethics and all races
being equal was a favourite joke. Do not
marry the Canaanite, smash the temple.

Sweet morning came with its starkness
and I continued my quest for spirituality,
seeking out the pagan, guided by angels.
Earth's song was singing to me once more,
a siren to 2 a.m. half-sleep and reality.

Into The Dream As I Once Strong
(The Light Of Dying)

Into the dream as I once strong,
cause my body to fade and, unwilling, gyrate,
spinning to the frail-mirrored room.
I fall to the stone-crowned floor
as, of light and crystal in robes,
the white-faced women circle and
take me unseen through crowds,
no blinding reflection in the liquid glass.

Now a casket marks my fall's place as I pass
and dulled, ceased life is how
the crystal shows itself as sand.
Pulsation from the light of strobes'
silver, hoping to restore
the heartbeat to this silent tomb,
escape from eumenides and reincarnate,
another dream, another form and tongue.

a reverse rhyme, from centre outwards

So Who Are You

So who are you
who was unknown
until you walked across the sea
to the land
(you claimed)

impregnated his wife
during a hectic schedule
by pulling just three times
and sending a jet of semen
through the open window
to the waiting egg
(you claimed)

who rules (most of) the world
and lets corporations
keep AIDS alive and well
in countries naturally weaker
and trade arms not alms
for stomachs to swell
with hunger
(unclaimed)

Reading Poetry

Settled in the shade of the high hedge,
bare-foot warmth from the holding concrete
by the mallow and house wall, I was
reading a couple of poems by Denise Blake.

Figures of neighbours chatted on the pavement.
"Fook'n cost eight hundred baarstards. Fook'n rip.
Droivin's a baarstard mugs game. Shits they are."
I was lying in the meadow with Denise,
somewhere in sunshine, somewhere in Ireland.
I stayed in Ireland with Daragh Breen,
walking my way to the pub on an icy road.
"…'n the 'angers-on fill the fook'n surgery
ev'ry Monday. Same fook'n faces. 'Ave toim
t'visit 'un if it weren't forrem. Shits they are."
Cornwall was in full summer, the seagulls inland
a little, following the farm trailer on the hill by
the flat Goonhilly Downs, easy, squabbled pickings.
"That work Ronnie or you jus' readin'?
Peaceful life y' ave there. Not loik uz 'un."

I travelled back into the book, to England, to America,
moving the wine bottle from the creeping sun,
searching for any sign of shits in my world.

Ack. Denise Blake Song
Daragh Breen No Great Mischief

Above Lies The Criss-cross Of Cloud Strands

(Poem In Summer)

Above lies the criss-cross of cloud strands
Where the sight of the eyes and ears' voices now mix
  With the playing wind from the green-hill
      Capturing
       Essence of summer
Ground-high and firm or waving on high afternoons
My trees frame the dark against the most purple sky
    Shield silent herds
      Galloways
Drifting as breeze disturbing nothing.

The flow that is the sound of sunshine
Covers the boundaries now smudged into summer
  Lilting voices lifting on warm air
      Beautiful
     And full of laughter
Carrying the legends in gossip wilderness
The majesty of nature chiselled in my heart
    History of stone
      Hewing
The ache that can occupy daydreams.

My body has soared with the buzzards
Porous skin prickled with the sheer joy of vision
   Shadows nestling the valley glow
            Beautiful
         Dappling bright places
Pouring premature night over silver-drenched gorse
Sun-high to resolute silhouette now as one
         Breathing pure spirit
            Exhaling
      The virtue of this blithe canvass land.

(…with all respect to DT….)

Phoenix Was Rising

Fragile Earth.
The balloon was in the baby's hand,
the butterfly was on the hedge
and the weary man asleep.

God – how we try to fight oppression
suppression, forced beliefs and control.
How we hate the tumbling brick walls,
the bones, concrete and flesh.
The tsunami of dust, memory, spirit.

Fragile Earth.
The song of a bird, low and hypnotic….
a sound of wings beating…..
then the fire.

Beautiful music, somehow pastoral,
in the heart of the city.
People claimed to have felt calm,
safe and at peace. Right there.
In the heart.

Come Away She Said

Come away she said
and I did, to the Logan Stone at
Porthcurno's indigo bay, swept
clean by the busy Atlantic, to find
her on the stage under Minack
Theatre stars, speaking of sharing
a world with wine and paintings;
to the isolation of Rame Peninsula,
where she said we were the only
people left alive; to the higgledy-piggledy
Polperro streets, where we lived in a
house on stilts, roaming the shadowy
wooded valley and counted the blacks,
silvers and blues in the harbour. We
drifted the Lerryn Creek, through the
water-meadows to the spire at Lostwithiel
Church, where we never married.
I crawled to find her under Heligan's
blanket of brambles, lost myself in
the jungle, seeking romance in the
Italian garden. I heard her voice echo
through the white yachts at Carrick Roads,
the towering magnolias of Trelissick.

Come away she said,
to the mists settling on the Manacle Rocks,
where she would guide me to the ocean
bed. Hazed in blue and unprepared, I fell
against the serpentine cathedral rocks
and cracked a water-drilled nugget to
the footprint sands. When it split, an inner
fossil contoured against the evening air.
It was then that I traced the outline of
her heart, so cold against my bloody hands.

Crop Circles

Crop circles are all fake,
with concentric alignment
the result of publicity-money
farmers, pub jokers.

Except the ones with that
stub, the burn, the charred
mark that all circle plants show,
which delineates each pattern
from where the crop continues
to grow. Not snapped; not ruined.
Growing.

And the farmers see and they
harvest, the product digested
by us, to stay cynics. And they
say it's a hoax, because their crop
is perfect. After followers, the field
ploughed.

(And the cows with the stripped lips,
drained blood and udders removed
with surgical precision, recorded eighty
per cent in just one area of America
just like the percentage of crop circles
recorded in the south-west of England.)

And in the south-west of England,
despite denials the first recordings
of stripped cows have just been
officially recognised. Same area.
Same percentage. Same joke.

Deep Night in the Smoky Life

Deep night in the smoky life;
the next alcove is just legs.

Below knees with bracelet hand,
full-coloured nails and two rings.

His blue deck-shoes are raised,
stoic, absorbing the ash from the

unattended manicured hand with
the half-ash tumbling disregarded.

Her raised foot is tapping unquestioned,
and delicate fingers spread on a distant knee.

Communication is from an unseen place,
nothing between the legs.

Evangelists With Badges, Pushers Of Faith

It was quite a walk to the church
that looked like a government building.
I was asked to sit in the wheelchair, then
kindly pushed inside so I could look up
to the many people gathered there. My
pusher gave me a badge, my protective
badge. He then wheeled me into a large
empty hall. The many people had walked
to the upper floor to overlook, to judge.

The wind blew, the mist rose and swirled,
spirits appeared, voodoo rising. I wheeled
my chair in vain circles, screaming, until
calm returned and I sat still, covered in vomit.

Pushed along to the preachers' hall I could
hear the whispers, 'where's his badge?' 'why
didn't he run?' 'what did he see?' One by one
the great men spoke. All as one we showed
devotion. To general chatter we emerged,
my clothes were clean, my badge restored.
The whisperers had noticed, impressed.
I paid my money, returned my badge and
rose from the chair, thanking the many people
standing there. Then I started quite a walk
away from the church.

Donna

On summer solstice by the water,
full green reflecting on the pond,
coots collecting bread for their young
and the sweet hum of June insects.
She came from across the Jerseys'
field, a thirty-year-old child, beautiful
and pure. Slightly troubled, she had
experienced another's death through
the ghost of the victim, seeing the wall,
feeling the regions of pain through
prickled skin. She told me without
embellishment, with a natural rush
and held hands as she described the
surge of warmth that filled her as he
finally passed over, and how doves
flew down to feed in her garden at
almost exactly the same time.

We were dowsing for reasons in sunlight
and I was comforting with presence.
Later, we watched fireworks over farms
and evening shadows grow longer from
the base of the stones. It all seemed
calm, perfectly calm, the breeze cleansing
in whispers, our only communication coming
inwardly, from the heart and the breath,
outwardly, with a positive flow of hands.

Fly Free

Bound and twisting,
the griffin lay in chains
until Alexander commanded flight.

And now, my sweet child
on the threshold of power,
I wait for your commands.

Leather bonds restrict resistance
as, prone to the bird of prey,
I lie for the lion.

Alexander tempted with meat
and the griffin flew
high in indolent flight.

To what temptation will you rise,
to compel that I rise
as I come to your commands?

 (I feel your breath
unstructured and stumbling,
soft flesh rubbing moist…..)

This is your time to devour,
to metamorphose your dreams
and take without condition.

And when you fly, fly free,
grip me in talons of fantasy,
show me the sweetest pain.
Fly free

Global Village

In this village are a hundred people
and fifty-two of the villagers are female.
Seventy are non-white, Seventy non-
Christian and seventy unable to read.
One in ten of them are homosexual
and sixty-per-cent of the whole village
is completely owned by just six people.
And these six people are all American.

Sadly, in this village, half are starving
and eighty have substandard housing.
On one side a person is dying;
on another side a person is pregnant.
Only one of us owns a computer
and only one of us has an education.
And you already live in this village -
a scaled down version of our world.

So perhaps when we wake up we can
think of fellow villagers who won't survive
the week. When we visit our god, or speak
freely, think of those who can't without
harassment, and torture. And see past
the news to the shadows. Fellow villagers
without a voice who need us, who somehow
must be heard. Even in their silence.

It's Just Another Day

Met Aleister Crowley at the Hermetic Order
and we visited La Vey at the Church of Satan.
He read from the Satanic Bible which was a laugh,

particularly the one about the virgin and the goat.
Feeling just somewhat shallow, saw Mary Baker Eddy,
and left, still feeling shallow but holistically poorer.

Tried to check the engrams in my body so
the little Thetan alien I'm the capsule for
would be healthy. Couldn't, so gave up with scientology.

Attended my marriage ceremony, organised by
Sun Myung Moon. I found him mesmeric and I'm
looking forward to a trance-like life of obedience.

It was the seventh day so I rested. Made notes for tomorrow:
Do dissertation on stupidity of lemmings.
Follow the little white rabbit down the hole.

Catalogue Men Wear Taupe

Sometimes the clouds of people cluster
and attack my inner being, so the world
is a fish-eye lens and each step has to be
so precise or fall. I am that strange man
with the ridiculous tread, sweating for no
good reason; who's forgotten his propanolol
or diazepam; who hears the voices echo
through the bucket; who's sense of space
is invaded. Prosody blends to paralinguistic
with the pace too fast and heartbeats trying
to keep pace; proxemics are ignored with
bodies passing inches from mine, unity and
protection breached. I must swim, sit, sink.

But I also have to remember to breathe correctly
with full use of the lung, the unused twenty percent.
The world's time-rush does not apply to me and
this piece of air is mine alone, this ground in
temporary possession. Then I can see the strength
in my being, my own water-skin so unique and apart,
no reason to join the rushing crowd as I'm happily
ignored and only catalogue men wear taupe. Yes.
Catalogue men wear taupe.

The Kiss

It seemed like a black frame but when
she'd done things to it, all you could
make out were highlighted corners
that seemed to drift off to Moroccan
covers, hanging deepest red against the
diffused white light and my eyes were
starting to go. Replace the art with the
South African box fruity and full 13%
that will go some way. The computer
has analysed the atmosphere to be gentle
with overtones of mistrust perfect for
experimental late nights, where people
seemed to be walking in colour before
we started and the window crystals were
giving whatever and more. The room was
revolving really early and we somehow had
to laugh. I recall her rubbing my bald head
with its spiky bits and it felt good. It felt
like a cuddle I'd been missing for ages but
she said it was a type of massage and I was
too tense. I think she felt the patient disappointing.
But maybe it was a sneak cuddle to me and she
was just multi-coloured pretending to disguise.
Somewhere softness in a black top approached
and it seemed an intrusiveness too soon, soft
sexual parts in contact but I felt the mystic far off
and lulled by the sitar felt compelled to stay and
drink in the breath of the girl with the black lashes,
breathe out some wild shore disregard with the hope
she'd say please don't stop this moment, something's

stirring and I'm normally so frozen in time, I'm
embryonic if someone will wrap me with towels
or arms that are soft as clouds. Mix my perfume
with wine-smoke, she said, and I was soon biting
gently on black lips that held black cherry, just
enough for me to keep licking, minutes after.
Wherever I touched was OK. My arms sometimes
guided by the others to find the soft and the warm.
She sat like a sculpture in creation while we fondled
with the essence of jasmine, the smoke of rose and held
our own courts together in the various areas of the rooms.
Her I must get to know, with the gentleness of pure
domination and a smile that leads to a bite on my lip,
then another, just pecking or sucking like a bird, smiling
back to me after each time. If I could kiss eyes, I would,
rub my tongue over brown sparkle, bring the cornered smile
to even greater heights. Minx. The brown has closed and just
parted lips with a look of please, but please what? She
doesn't move. She just waits and slowly I place a finger on
her lips. Then she moves, rolls her lips and takes it slowly, so
gently between her teeth, they saw and bite without mark and
I feel I know her. With her, intrusive hands were not so
much of a distance, were part of the lips which later were
employed intimately, and soft, delicate areas were held kissed
and sucked.
The game for two, no noise, no noise. Each hand on her
body was delicate at the far end of her cloth, the touch so
light to excite and arouse, ask for more contact, heavier, even
rougher. As she stood to her full height, she decided to kiss,
still gently, but properly with contact for some time and with
the haze and the scent of her my arms misbehaved, moving
and moving to where baser instincts took, gentle, yes, but
investigating, resolving to add to the kiss with sighs,
squeezes,

movement that she couldn't control, so for a short while she was mine, ready to respond to the actions I took and maybe, maybe the words that I said. Her arms around my neck, her black hair in my face, where I'd love to smell it, to taste it. And then the moist eyes through tousled hair looking up and telling that was a fabulous kiss.

That's all she ever wanted,
a fabulous kiss.
She thanked me so much. Then said goodbye.

Chemical Purity

So it's probably best if we leave
the citalopram and forget seroxat,
maintain allopurinol for the joints,
dispersible aspirin every morning
too, together of course, with your
metformin for diabetes. Only take
the diclofenac when the pain gets
too much. In the evening make sure
you take the metformin again, the
simvastatin and the zolpidem when
you feel it's essential. We'll have
the sleep apnoea results in a month
or so. You'll probably have to strap
up to a machine for life, though.

There we are then. It must be
great for you out at Predannack.
All that beauty and pure air.
Must clear your head for poetry

Lizard Friday

It was one of those really shit situations,
you with two pints of Scrumpy Jack and
a Rottweiller nosing a Doberman on the
floor, right between you and your table.

But it's OK, because the girl in blue says
they are both SO misunderstood and the
growl is because of my uncertainty. They
can smell it, even at a bar where all's cool.

And at the bar Serpentine bar-pull regales
mis-matches trying to make it right over a pint.
This slightly-backward girl is making decisions
and the two accompanists are seeking reasons.

The walker says he's now done the whole coast,
and he's talking about his home targets as if game,
not the home that I actually live in season to season
and adapt to it's wild and its off-peak beauty.

The bloke reading Phil Cornwell tries to talk,
but beyond the ordering of food and false laughs
there's nothing. The bar has closed Cornish ranks.
He picks at his envied crab-meat, dabs his mouth.

So I got to talk and he's selling his house to sail on
his boat to another life. Lost his wife, slowly recovered;
lost his dog, and that was the final straw. No love left;
Going off to the sunset with sadness, money and a puppy.

The pretty woman is moaning about her cleaner;
she's big-titted in black with a blaze of red from her
jeans. Her friends are muted as she says something
about gardens and kitchens; she's talking pants.

And the older man takes the subnormal for a meal,
intentions unquestioned; and the moaner is talking
to a teen-plus who knows when the husband is home
and they agree it hurts no-one as long as it's secret.

I've got the fag-end of my cider left, the bus'll be pulling
to the village green in about eight minutes. The eating
girl's looking for a friend that isn't there. The husband's
treated like a ghost at the bar. I catch the last bus for home.

Music On Computers

1)

And the good old boys coming back
from the Old Inn, the village quiet, the
back road a whisper, the piling into
the cottage a squabble of the ending joke
and the new quiet. Computer on for the
retained music, Bob Dylan chosen as homage
to this guest, busy with wine corks, plastic
and real, dry cider bottles fizzing with a
fresh-bubble fizz and Joanne, waiting by
the sink with a smile and a confidence,
knowing the juice is in the fridge door,
the spirits on the floor of the bedroom,
by the uplighter. We pecked a kiss, another.

And the flavour was Just Like A Woman and
John and Jeremy were holding court in the hall
that formed the dining room and sometimes spread
the lounge, depending on warm or cold weather.
And there's me, holding the smoke, grinning on the
terracotta throw of their cheap settee, pillows as
cushions and comfy. And Jane sinks in too. Terribly
friendly, adult, with her old dad my friend a next
drink away. So she kisses and I falter, she makes a
presence and I tell her diabetes affects in many ways.
Her hand presses and tells me I seem unaffected.

So we're on the settee, I've joined a few conversations
and the agarbati is smelling wonderful. Joanne has pecked
me in the kitchen and holding court with Lizard ladies,
full of country and fishing and sex. And sex with gossip.
She puts my hand on her tits. I feel nothing, so show
her by finding and fighting my way through tight sewing
and designer bra. No room. What's more is the singing
to 'Hey' Mr Tambourine Man, with a big call on the 'hey' bit.
The room is alive behind me and it's Dylan calling the
chorus.
Personally, I went for 'tambourine.' Emphasis was big with
me.
I was definitely a 'tambourine' man.

2)

The walls are a kind of orange, that colour that
always looks better than it sounds. Covered in
Indian throws, with a few of my own sketches,
framed for importance, and a print of a poet
smoking pot somewhere in the sixties. And there's
this block print of Leighton Jones 'Artful Dodger',
so perfect with its look that it'll fit in nowhere,
scruffy painting and a pipe-smoking kid. I'd take
him in. But she's more serious this time. And I'm
more vulnerable – weaker is the word – than
ever. Totally alone, I know these walls, just some
Joni to change the scene, and she sighs too. Too much.

It's a great sweaty time with no love but lust proving
that the flavour of each moment can be as sweet or
sour as you wish it. She was newer than me, riding
from the top and looking at me with eyes displaying
she was somewhere else, dancing with me under
moonlight, screwing in some alleyway, thrusting
her bum in some field. No romance here, just some
stolen moment to later forget, just smells of each other,
a kind of perfumed sex, but lovely tonight.

3)

The big issue in the follow-up - 'did I have you or
did you have me?' Seems there's this thing that there's
always someone who brings the other one off. And
there's me been at it for thirty years and didn't
know a thing about it. I pictured one of these flashback
times where in a dream-like image my past came forward
and I lost like 40-nil or maybe, 70-nil, or maybe....
So I told her she was the one, I couldn't hold back,
I couldn't function again for hours. Strangely, she didn't
ask for how many hours or how I knew that. I was going
to say once upon a time I made love. But I didn't.

So back here among the scents and the music and the
people and the thoughts she said to me 'have we finished?'
Isn't it funny how the music stops, the room goes into
a bucket. Dylan, Mitchell, Morrison, Cohen, but could
I find a rhyme? Joanne took me to the cottage lounge.
Hugged me, danced to Brown Eyed Girl, I told her I'd
like to spend my life with her. She smelled of the future
from some designer bottle, but it was the taste of my
love. 'No chance' was the wonderful smiled whisper.
I fell in love with that too, it's just the way the heart runs.
I didn't mean it either, just running the red wine haze.

4)

It was a good few years since my divorce, many more
since that play that makes you whole or leaves your
inner being screaming ' what's the point, what's the
fucking point…' and on a much lesser scale, I enjoyed
being taken on a settee, among the incense, music,
candlelight and laughter of our making. Bohemian
swansong? Probably. But her dad's here tonight and
he's on great form. One of the characters emerged
that weren't heroes of the war. He brags of nothing,
but he shines, like his daughter, unpredictable, but
welcome on any settee. We had a poetry and folk
night, seven of us in tune sometime but eventually
out of it.

Some weeks later in the cool night and walking, he
said how she was quite abandoned in many ways
impractical in others but always left this spark behind,
this longing and she'd always come back when you'd
started to settle. That feeling in your stomach and heart
would rise again and off you'd go on another gypsy night.
And here she was again, running from the track with the
faintest trail of dust rising and a shimmer like diamonds
on stones. Almost a perfume too. Almost. 'What brings
you here?' he grinned. 'Him?' 'No' she said, 'music on
computers.' We both looked suitably confused. 'OK.
Bye Ronnie, bye Joanne, enjoy your music.'

5)

Somewhere deep in her terracotta throws, scattered
like a womb, she hugged a satin cushion, Indian,
ornate, dubious quality, smelling wonderfully of
sandalwood and her. I guided her machine to
the right spot, found the switch to make her senses
rise and her body drift from the space where her green
eyes peeped through, beautiful but cold, shining without
depth, luring again to the temptation of insecurity. No
reality here, or suspended for a while. What would Jane
have thought if she'd been there? I'd explain it's just
machine love, the only sort that's left. Powered like music
on computers. Yes. Let's call it music on computers